Millennial Managers & Gen Z Employees

VAISHNAVI AGRAWAL

BLUEROSE PUBLISHERS
India | U.K.

Copyright © Vaishnavi Agrawal 2025

All rights reserved by author. No part of this publication may be reproduced, stored in a retrieval system or transmitted in any form or by any means, electronic, mechanical, photocopying, recording or otherwise, without the prior permission of the author. Although every precaution has been taken to verify the accuracy of the information contained herein, the publisher assumes no responsibility for any errors or omissions. No liability is assumed for damages that may result from the use of information contained within.

BlueRose Publishers takes no responsibility for any damages, losses, or liabilities that may arise from the use or misuse of the information, products, or services provided in this publication.

For permissions requests or inquiries regarding this publication, please contact:

BLUEROSE PUBLISHERS
www.BlueRoseONE.com
info@bluerosepublishers.com
+91 8882 898 898
+4407342408967

ISBN: 978-93-7018-600-2

Cover design: Yash Singhal
Typesetting: Namrata Saini

First Edition: May 2025

To my parents, for their unwavering support.

To my friends, for their encouragement.

And to my sister, Aditi—for always being my calm and compass

Preface

The workplace is changing—fast. As new generations enter the corporate world, long-standing norms are being questioned, redefined, and, in some cases, completely overturned. The conversations happening in office corridors, Zoom meetings, and leadership discussions today are unlike those of a decade ago. At the heart of these shifts lies an intriguing dynamic: the evolving relationship between millennial managers and Gen Z employees.

Having spent years working alongside professionals from both generations, I've seen firsthand the misunderstandings, the friction, and—most importantly—the untapped potential of this evolving workplace dynamic. Millennials, once the disruptors, now find themselves in leadership positions, navigating the expectations of a workforce that values flexibility, purpose, and open communication more than ever before. Gen Z, in turn, is bringing fresh perspectives and bold ideas but often clashes with traditional corporate structures.

This book is not about pitting one generation against the other. It is about understanding why these differences exist, where they stem from, and how they can be transformed into strengths rather than sources of conflict. Through insights drawn from real experiences, industry trends, and shifting workplace behaviours, Millennial Managers & Gen Z Employees explores how businesses and individuals can bridge the generational divide to create a workplace that works for everyone.

If you've ever wondered why workplace dynamics feel different today, why certain leadership styles no longer resonate, or how to make intergenerational collaboration more effective, you are in for a treat. Whether you're a manager trying to lead a team, an employee navigating your career, or simply someone curious about the future of work, I invite you to join me in unpacking the evolving corporate landscape—one conversation at a time.

Contents

1.) Perception of Work 1
2.) The Office 13
3.) The Corporate Ladder 26
4.) Beyond 9 to 5 36
5.) More than Money 49
6.) Redefining Dream Jobs 67
7.) Way Ahead 78
About the Author 91
Bibliography 93
Acknowledgments 95

1.) Perception of Work

When we talk about corporate jobs today, it's impossible to ignore the two generations shaping their present and future—Millennials and Gen Z. As evident from the title, these are the focus generations of this book—not just because they dominate the workforce, but because their views on ambition, balance, and purpose often clash, and at times, align in fascinating ways. Why have we chosen these two generations in particular? We'll explore that in the chapters ahead. For now, let's delve into how each of them perceives work in their lives—and how those perceptions differ.

Work, whether it is your salaried job, your own business, or your passion project, accounts for one of the most prominent aspects of your life. And how can the presumably 40-hour-a-week part of your life not be important? It definitely is! But the question here is, how important? Is work one aspect of your life, an important aspect but just one aspect of your life or your entire life? People wouldn't normally admit to the latter but that is the case for many. How do you know which case is true for you? Ask yourself for a 40-hr work week (maybe more) how much are you actually dedicating to your work, is there anything else you're actively pursuing apart from work regularly? It can be a hobby, a fitness goal, or even quality time with your partner. Are you doing this? Ask yourself if you are constantly thinking about your work even when you are free, if you are out for a good run are the problems at work the first thing you think about? Well, this was the case for me. Even on my way home from work, I would be drafting the emails I needed to send out in my head. I had to remind myself that I was off the clock and that I should actually be thinking about whether I should do my laundry or make dinner first.

Once you've reflected on these questions, you'll start to see a pattern emerge. Work has different meanings to different people, but for many, it becomes more than just a part of life—it becomes the very core of their identity. This is especially true for millennial managers, whose approach to work is deeply rooted in generational values. Given the age dynamics in a country like India, a majority is bound to be married or be a family man or actively looking to settle down. It's just the provider instinct that makes work a top priority, without them even realizing it. I think it all stems from the idea of and need to be the "provider".

Let's take the example of my father, a typical Gen X, the way he worships his work is out of this world and certainly out of my understanding. Back when the standard of living of a majority of Indians wasn't very high, Indian middle-class men took it upon themselves to do their hardest to provide for their families. And where did they bring us? They gave us a more comfortable life, more than they could ever have. That led to the future generation having a better start in life, from the massive competition for private school admissions to corporate internships through your father's contacts, it was a big leap. If we take a step back and see, the millennial managers also took up the same mentality without considering the benefits they had already received.

Another aspect to look at here is education, the older generations were not very educated and hence focused a lot on their child getting a good education in schools, getting into good colleges, working for an MNC, and getting a job that gets them home by 6 and gives you Saturdays and Sundays off to enjoy with your family. This was the dream! Maybe not exactly this but you get the idea. This was still the dream they sought for their children so that they'd have to toil less than their fathers and forefathers.

As the Indian economy shifted from an agriculture-based economy to a service-based economy, the prideful corporate era commenced. With this came the hard work and struggles to land that reputable corporate job and the urge to make your family proud. This meant focusing all your energy and attention on that one goal. Keeping in mind there weren't a lot of options and distractions back then, focusing on your one ultimate goal was the first step towards the inevitable success. With less focus on extracurriculars and little exposure to technology when they were growing up, they went all in for academics. And that's what they learned, focusing everything on the most important thing in your life that leads to financial freedom and acceptance in society. The one thing that makes your parents proud. The one thing they can boast about at dinner parties. With this relentless pursuit of excellence, an entire generation grew up believing that success was a linear path—good academics leading to a great job, which in turn secured their future. But as work took centre stage in their lives, a crucial question remained unanswered: Is this approach sustainable in a rapidly evolving world? They developed tunnel vision, the light at the end of this tunnel shined as bright as their beaming and inevitable success and the end of the tunnel is their job.

The millennials became the breadwinner of their family and eventually raised the yardstick against which educated people were measured. Be it for new opportunities or marriage prospects, a good job gives you all of it! With this, the millennials started chasing the best. Just doing something wasn't enough now, doing it from the "best" institution was what they needed to do. They wanted to get the best college, the best job, the best next job, and so on. And they did! But this hardworking and heart-wrenching quest made them yearn more not just for themselves but also for the people around them, including their juniors. They believe they have worked really hard to get where they are (they must have) but the newer generations have it too easy. They don't have to toil as much to reach the same places. Somewhere they feel the newer generations need to be penalized for having it too easy. So, they carried forward the "work is life" philosophy that they learned from their seniors. Give in extra hours, make an extra effort, please your boss, treat the team as your family, and of course, just like a family, don't expect anything in return. But, is this the right way to approach things? Wasn't having things easy for the coming generations the whole point?

Let's talk about how Gen Z perceives work. We'll take a step back again and see how our parents brought us up. By the time we were in school, education wasn't just a desire anymore—it became a necessity, no longer an option but a fundamental requirement Everyone your age around you is educated. Now how will their child set themselves apart? How will they outshine themselves for those fancy corporate jobs now? How will they define success and set themselves apart from their peers?

They need other extracurriculars that make them a well-rounded individual and not just a bookworm. Activities that make them interesting and give them experiences that they can talk about with their colleagues in the future. Maybe pick up a sport, or music or dance, or maybe writing, something was needed to fill that gap. This was when the school-going, homework-burdened students were exposed to multiple things at the same time. Go to school, then tuition for better scores, then your dance or karate classes or your basketball practice, after that let's do your homework and why not read a book before bed or watch a documentary to make you even more interesting and develop cognitive reading capabilities. Why not? Let's do it. And we did it.

We somehow overdid it. But what was the silver lining here? We learned how to manage multiple things at once, and how to navigate and prioritize our work while balancing our personal lives. Because no one missed the TV watching hour no matter how much homework we had or how tired we were. Basically, we learned how even after 20 tasks a day, you can find that one hour where you do you.

Thinking about it now, it might have been the best thing I subconsciously learned along the way. Ultimately, we learned to prioritize from a life perspective and not a work perspective. This ideology came with us throughout our lives. Even in college, we juggled studies internships, college events, and of course the god-forbidden extracurriculars. And now when we are in corporate, life with just work feels empty. We often have the desire to do more in our daily routine just as we have been taught growing up. So, what do we do? We prioritize new skills, new experiences, new workout regimes, and new hobbies, all of this unrelated and outside work. Giving us opportunities and interests we would want to pursue outside of work. Making work is just another aspect of our well-rounded lives.

Who is to say which perception is right or wrong? But one thing is for sure, the company and its representative would always want you to make work your top priority while at the same time preaching about the importance of work-life balance. This leads to a coherent battle in your mind where you would need to make the right choice every day. Every day you'll need to choose your fitness goals and hobbies over your work and sneak some time out for yourself. Every day you'll need to choose family time wrap up your work before dinner and give your attention to your family. This eccentric circle of choices is actually what exhausts us. From being capable of juggling multiple things at once to not being able to decide if your work will be over on time so you can grab some drink with your friends, it takes a toll on all of us.

I am not saying you always have to juggle multiple things in life. Not everyone needs to. But no matter what, giving time to yourself should be on the to-do list for everyone, every day. If not, it wouldn't be late when you ask yourself, why are we doing this?

Going back to how our father's generation sacrificed everything for work- for us. Wasn't the whole point to make things easy for us and for us to not have the same struggles? After decades, we now need to prioritize the things our parents couldn't do to truly honour their contributions to our lives. For this, the first step is to give yourself the time you deserve. How do we do it? By realizing that your work needs you as much as you need it. By not making it your life. By taking that much-needed break and by setting boundaries.

This is how the perception of work differs across generations. It is only going to change furthermore as we advance in terms of social structures and technology. As the "acceptable accordion" for the society definition widens, the gap is bound to increase. What we need to focus on is, if this gap is hampering someone's career, productivity, or mental health. A few decades down the line when we won't be able to encapsulate how our younger generation works, we'll need a reminder of how we positioned ourselves and what we are expecting from our millennial managers right now, would be what our juniors seek from us.

This difference in perception of the same work can largely be the inception of differences between ideologies and ideas and also how you approach things. When we talk about the corporate world, this can also lead to different adaptations of your performance. You might feel like you gave it all and gone beyond expectations, but your millennial manager might have different plans. This leads to startling performance ratings and feedback which in turn affects your compensation and thereby decreasing your zeal to work harder and out-perform. In companies where appraisals and bonuses are directly linked to your performance, having a middle manager who disregards hard work in terms of how often you come to the office or how well your relationship with them or the team is, will doom your time at the organization.

What was once considered hard work and a path to success is merely considered a means to make a living. "My son works at an MNC" isn't as glamorous as it used to be. Because now the response would be, "So is mine" instead of "Oh! How lucky!" There's just nothing to set you apart anymore if your entire life and personality revolves around your work. Because guess what, everyone's working and making a living, maybe more than you with fewer hours to work.

This doesn't mean you shouldn't go beyond expectations at work—you absolutely should. However, before fully devoting yourself to your job, take a step back to analyse what truly contributes to excellent performance and what genuinely propels you to the next level. Is it just a fleeting work-worship fad, or is it the real learning and growth you achieve?

You need to understand the performance metrics of your organization and critically evaluate whether these metrics are genuinely used to measure your contributions and those of your colleagues—or if they're merely a façade to glorify the person who stays late at the office or takes on the workload of five people single-handedly.

While these individuals may be considered an asset to the company, they often end up undervalued because they've already given their all and have little left to offer to perpetually demanding roles. Managers, having seen their peak performance, may push them further to test their limits—often leading to burnout and mental exhaustion.

In the end, the generational divide in the perception of work boils down to priorities, upbringing, and the evolution of societal norms. While Millennials often equate hard work and overcommitment with success, Gen Z approaches work with a more balanced lens, seeking purpose and sustainability. Neither perspective is inherently right or wrong—they are reflections of their respective environments and experiences. What's crucial is promoting an understanding between these generations to bridge this gap in the workplace. Organizations must evolve to recognize the value of diverse work styles, ensuring that performance metrics reward meaningful contributions rather than glorifying overwork.

As individuals, the burden lies on us to strike a balance between ambition and self-preservation. To honour the sacrifices of those before us, we must prioritize what they couldn't: our well-being, our passions, and the time we give to ourselves and our loved ones. By setting boundaries and embracing the broader picture of life, we redefine success—not as a measure of hours worked, but as a testament to a fulfilling, multidimensional life. Only then can we truly thrive in an ever-changing corporate environment and ensure that the workplace evolves with us, not against us. This will not only make us happier at work but willing to work to the best of our capabilities and stick longer in the same organization.

2.) The Office

The modern office is a diverse space, filled with individuals from multiple generations, each bringing unique perspectives, skills, and beliefs to the workplace. From the seasoned Gen X directors to the ambitious millennial managers and the tech-savvy Gen Z analysts, the workplace is a melting pot of different values, communication styles, and work ethics. While each generation has its own distinct traits, they all carve out their own niches—forming friendships, building careers, and contributing to the company's success in different ways. This book delves into the dynamics between two of these generations—millennials and Gen Z—highlighting their differences, similarities, and the evolving nature of work. We focus our discussion on Millennials and Gen Z because managers, predominantly Millennials, are part of the corporate hierarchy that Gen Z interacts with most frequently and looks up to for guidance. The generational gap between Gen X and Gen Z is significantly wider, making it less relatable for direct workplace dynamics. Millennials, having already worked to bridge the gap with Gen X, now find themselves in a vital role of establishing common ground with Gen Z. So, we begin by examining the millennial managers and Gen Z employees, shedding light on how their values, work preferences, and expectations shape the modern corporate environment.

Gen Z in corporate is fairly different from the other generations of corporate employees we have seen so far. The Zurich Insurance Group estimates that Gen Z will make up almost 27% of the total corporate workforce by 2025. They are definitely reshaping the entire landscape! Born literally at the cusp of a new century, Gen Z is the most diverse generation today. They are progressive, activist-minded, and well aware of their rights. They know the power their voices hold and aren't shy about being heard. They know the change they want in the corporate world, and they are actively driving that change.

To truly understand Gen Z's approach to work, we need to examine what sets them apart from their predecessors. Unlike previous generations, they challenge traditional workplace ideologies and reject corporate norms that no longer align with their reality. One such belief is the notion of 'work as a family'—a sentiment they actively push against. Recent large-scale layoffs across top companies have only served to reinforce the idea that work is not family.

Between 2022 and 2023, Microsoft laid off 1,900 employees, Google cut 12,000 jobs, and Nokia slashed 14,000 roles—proof that even the most powerful corporations prioritize numbers over people. Companies preaching "work is family" are often the first to lay off their "beloved" employees. In an era where even familial trust isn't blind, expecting unwavering loyalty to capitalist, ever-changing, and often ruthless organizations seems paradoxical.

For Gen Z, job security is no longer a given, and they are adapting accordingly. They refuse to clock in hours just for the sake of appearances. Instead, they seek autonomy over their time, valuing efficiency over outdated notions of workplace dedication. This pragmatic approach has made job-hopping a norm rather than an exception.

A 2021 report by CareerBuilder, one of the largest job search platforms in the US, found that Gen Z employees spend an average of 2.3 years in a single role—far shorter than the 4.6 years of baby boomers and 3.4 years of millennials. This shift reflects a generation unwilling to stay in stagnant roles, especially when employers show no long-term commitment to their workforce.

Similarly, a 2023 study by Oliver Wyman, conducted across the US and UK, revealed that Gen Z doesn't associate frequent job changes with career instability—a stark contrast to previous generations who saw long tenures as a sign of reliability. Nearly 70% of Gen Z respondents in the study stated they would leave a job if it no longer aligned with their values or personal goals, even if they had no immediate alternative lined up.

This growing detachment from the traditional employer-employee dynamic is not a sign of recklessness but rather a conscious shift in workplace expectations. Gen Z prioritizes career fluidity, personal fulfilment, and adaptability—traits that can either be a challenge or a competitive advantage for millennial managers, depending on how they choose to navigate them.

This willingness to move on speaks volumes about their resilience and pragmatism. They're not inclined to wait around for things to improve or for companies to gradually warm up to the generation's needs. They're proactive, taking the next step when necessary. They understand that while they need jobs, the job market also needs their skills, creativity, and innovative perspectives.

Gen Z's job-hopping tendencies reflect their broader philosophy on work—one that prioritizes fulfilment over longevity. But beyond their willingness to move on, their workplace expectations extend further, particularly in terms of authenticity and work-life balance. They're less likely to tolerate performative workplace culture and prefer environments that align with their values. They're vocal about mental health and expect organizations to prioritize it, too. Flexible work arrangements, inclusive policies, and meaningful engagement are not just perks for this generation—they're expectations.

Moreover, Gen Z is redefining the relationship between work and personal identity. They seek roles that resonate with their values and purpose. Unlike prior generations that often-equated professional success with stability and hierarchy, Gen Z places equal importance on personal fulfilment and societal impact. They are digitally native, growing up in an era of rapid technological advancements, and they use these skills to bring efficiency and innovation to the workplace. However, they also demand that companies keep up with technology and provide tools that enable productivity and creativity.

Gen Z's approach to corporate life is a reflection of their experiences, values, and the rapidly changing world they've grown up in. They are reshaping corporate norms, challenging outdated practices, and setting new standards for engagement and impact. They have unprecedented technological knowledge and an unmatched skillset. This generation isn't just participating in the corporate world—they're transforming it. And yet, this is just the beginning. There's much more to explore about how they are influencing industries, leadership styles, and workplace dynamics. The story of Gen Z in the corporate world is still unfolding, and the impact they are set to create will likely redefine the future of work as we know it.

When we talk about Millennial managers, they are a generation well into their 30s, often balancing family responsibilities, planning for the future, or even contentedly living independently. This is the cohort that has witnessed it all—from the evolution of mobile phones in their palms to the relentless demand to adapt to new technologies every year. They entered the job market at a time when mastering

Microsoft Excel which was once a standout, is now a basic necessity. I distinctly recall my millennial cousins investing in certified courses for Excel, while my school curriculum included it as a standard subject. Similarly, while I pursued a Python certification in college, my Gen Alpha cousin already has Python in her school syllabus. This generational shift is inevitable, and today, crafting effective prompts for AI assistants is one of the most valued skills for analysts and consultants. Did anyone foresee this being the case? Highly unlikely.

This evolution underscores the significant differences between Gen Z employees and their Millennial managers. Gen Z employees are acutely aware of the value they bring to the workplace, and they are unafraid to set boundaries. They expect their managers to recognize and leverage their efficiency. While some Millennial managers excel at this, others, struggling to adapt, may find themselves outpaced. Millennials, shaped by the hustle culture, often overwork and inadvertently expect the same from their employees. I am not denying the efficacy of the hustle culture, but I believe it suits the founders and business owners who also get to reap the benefits of each extra hour they put in, having the same expectations from a salaried employee is bewildering. Whenever the 90-hour workweek debates surface on the internet, it is quite a kerfuffle. In my opinion, doing a 40-hour work week along with something that keeps you upskilled is a valuable hustle at its core. I do not think the hustle culture denotes overworking or worshiping your job rather than making sure you do not waste your 20s partying but rather upskilling, networking, and building wealth. This is something up and aware Gen Z is already doing.

This contrast in work expectations between Millennials' deeply ingrained hustle culture and Gen Z's prioritization of efficiency becomes increasingly apparent. Will the workplace truly fall apart if an employee takes a few days off to prioritize mental health or simply to recharge? The answer is almost always no. I recall an incident when a friend confided in me about her struggles with mental health at work. When she expressed her concerns to her seniors, they dismissed her, suggesting she lacked time-management skills. When she sought support from others, she was formally warned against spreading "false rumours" or exaggerating her workload. This, despite routinely working 12-hour days, enduring weekend "important client calls," and taking almost no time off to avoid being judged. How long did she stay in this toxic environment? Four months. She moved on to a better-paying role with hopefully improved mental health support and senior management.

Such incidents, unfortunately, are not rare. They are often dismissed as easily as casual remarks from colleagues when employees leave on time, establish boundaries, or choose not to engage in workplace fraternization. This discussion isn't merely about the lack of empathy in corporate dynamics; it's about the critical need for managers to reassess how they engage with their teams. A manager cannot expect employees to replicate their own career journeys. Instead, they must cultivate a more interpersonal and empathetic environment that aligns with the evolving workforce.

Millennial managers also find themselves at a crossroads, juggling traditional expectations of leadership with the demands of a younger, more vocal workforce. For many, leadership was taught as a directive role, where authority was unquestionable, and the focus was on results above all else. However, this approach often clashes with Gen Z's expectations for collaboration, feedback, and flexibility. To bridge this gap, managers must embrace a more inclusive leadership style—one that values diverse perspectives and stimulates open communication.

Another key challenge for Millennial managers is adapting to the technological fluency of Gen Z. While Millennials had to learn technology incrementally,

Gen Z grew up with it, making them instinctive users of digital tools. This dynamic can create friction if managers feel threatened or fail to leverage their team's tech-savvy capabilities. Instead of resisting change, effective managers recognize the opportunity to learn from their younger employees, encouraging an environment of mutual growth.

Mental health awareness is another area where Millennial managers must step up. The stigma around discussing mental health in the workplace is gradually fading, thanks to Gen Z's insistence on prioritizing well-being. Managers who dismiss these concerns risk alienating their teams and raising high turnover rates. On the other hand, those who actively support mental health initiatives—through policies like flexible working hours, wellness programs, and open dialogue—build loyalty and trust within their teams.

Millennial managers often face the challenge of balancing productivity with empathy. Growing up in a hustle culture, they're used to putting results first, sometimes at the cost of well-being. However, the changing workplace environment calls for a shift in this approach. Managers who focus on teamwork, recognize achievements, and address challenges early on are more likely to create a positive and supportive work culture.

The role of Millennial managers is pivotal in bridging the generational gap. They are uniquely positioned, having experienced a corporate world that values hierarchy and hard work while now managing a generation that prioritizes authenticity, flexibility, and mental well-being. To succeed, Millennial managers must embrace adaptability and empathy, enabling workplaces where diversity of thought and experience are celebrated. By blending their resilience and experience with the fresh perspectives of Gen Z, they can create dynamic, forward-thinking teams that thrive in an ever-changing corporate environment.

While this perspective doesn't apply to everyone, it does highlight common workplace tendencies among different employees. Some Gen Z professionals, fully immersed in their work, push themselves to the limit in their early 20s, eager to maximize their potential, climb the corporate ladder, or build something of their own. They thrive in fast-paced environments, often taking on multiple projects, side hustles, or additional certifications to gain an edge. Their ambition is fuelled by a desire for early success, financial independence, and the flexibility that comes with achieving their goals sooner rather than later.

On the other hand, you may come across Millennials who, after years of grinding in high-pressure environments, have reached a point where they prioritize stability and personal well-being over chasing every promotion. Some have endured the hustle culture of their early careers, learned from their burnout, and now choose to approach work with a more measured perspective. There are those who do the bare minimum required to keep their jobs—just enough to get by, much like paying only the minimum amount due on their credit cards. These individuals may not be as driven by constant professional growth but rather focus on maintaining a steady pay check while directing their energy toward personal pursuits, family, or simply enjoying life outside of work.

Neither approach is inherently right or wrong. The goal here isn't to judge but to recognize the different mindsets at play in the workplace. Whether you relate to the Gen Z employees giving their all in an attempt to prove themselves, the Millennials maintaining a careful balance, or you find yourself somewhere in between, understanding these dynamics can help you navigate workplace interactions more effectively. If you don't identify with either group, this perspective still allows you to better interpret the behaviours, work ethics, and reactions of your colleagues, ultimately fostering a more collaborative and empathetic work environment.

Now that we have seen how the two generations differ in their dexterity, and how their views on work itself reveal an even deeper contrast. Let's take a closer look at how these perspectives affect their career trajectory.

3.) The Corporate Ladder

Having understood the perspectives of both generations, we can see how differently they see the corporate ladder. The corporate ladder is an interesting phenomenon. You put in the work, you put in the time, you put in the efforts, you reap the rewards. What are these rewards? More money, more benefits, better social circles, and more respect. Who doesn't want that? Aren't these benefits why we have been toiling so hard? Absolutely yes. But there's a lot that goes in.

Climbing the corporate ladder boils down to three things: work, time, and effort—each carrying its own weight in promotions and evaluations. Let's take a deeper look into this. When we talk about putting in the work, it means how well you do your job, how efficient you are in terms of deadlines, and how much you contribute to the actual growth of the company. In other words, how well do you score on the predetermined performance measurement parameters? There are some common themes across companies today that are used for employee performance measurement and feedback. They usually include: Quality of work, Quantity of work, Job knowledge and skills, and Working relationships. Essentially it means at the end of the year do you rank 1/5 or 4/5? (5 being the highest). Of course, 5/5 is a far-fetched dream people rarely attain. Anyways, this one-digit number pretty much summarises your 365 days of work and determines your worth.

When we look at time, we count both the hours you have put in and the years you have serviced. The hours component basically counts for the minimum number of hours being fulfilled, how many of them were billable, or how much revenue you generate per hour. Honestly, they rarely ever account for the extra hours you have worked, the days when you logged in early or the days when you pulled an all-nighter. If you work less than 40 hrs a week that's a no-no, however, if you work for 50+ hours, "Kudos, for doing your job". It's harsh but true. The years component attests to your loyalty to the company and dedication to your job. If you switch jobs too soon, it is a question of your commitment to your career before it becomes a question about the culture of the company or the lessons its management proclaims. Each promotion comes with a set of milestones that don't only account for the work you have done but also the years you need to achieve it. This is why new-age startups do not value tenure over talent and I believe this is a trend that is going to stay.

By efforts we mean, going beyond your job description, that one step to set you apart from your peers. It can range from how many extra activities you participated in; how many initiatives you took to how well you got with your team. All of this count and you either reap the benefits of these extra efforts or get punished for not doing enough.

When we look at this from the point of view of a millennial manager, the way to being promoted is to put in more work than you are required to, eventually leading to more hours every day and that stands as a good example of effort for them. Going beyond the job description isn't 'extra effort'—it's just the baseline expectation. Overwork isn't rewarded, it's assumed. For them, efforts like team building exercises or helping your peers do not count. Why? Because isn't this what you are supposed to do anyway? Isn't this company your family? Do you not want to be an important wheel driving this company? Do you not want to be seen? All these questions lead to only one answer- you cannot win in such a scenario unless you worship your work.

As we discussed before, Millennial managers started working when phones were barely in the market. Forget hybrid work, A lot of them learned about computers on their job, and got to experience the office life that we have seen in old movies. They grew from a point where punching in 5 minutes late meant you lose half a day's salary to a point where companies that have flexible working hours and they cannot shut up about it. Evidently, this was a long distance to cover. Going to the office every day sounds like a nightmare to me, but they did it. Effortlessly so. All these era-appropriate hardships seem like a lot for them. But weren't we looking up to a future where robots do everything for us? And aren't we getting closer to this dream by the day? Then why is there the need to penalize the ones who were born in the easier generations?

"In my early career days, we manually filled in Excel cells from a piece of paper. It sometimes took days to complete a report. Today AI will do everything for you and make your task so easy". That sounds tough. The next generation is always going to have it too easy. In the ever-evolving world, where technology has taken over the corporate world, it's high time we stop comparing generational hardships and judging the younger generations because of it. This is as ridiculous as saying, "I didn't have Instagram when I grew up. You shouldn't use it either" Just doesn't make any sense. But the truth is, this is how millennial managers compare performances and judge your work ethic.

Things on the outer side of the job, as in hiring and employment are easily affected as generations change. There used to be jobs for tasks like typing, translating, data entry, etc which are rarely seen today. Why? Everyone has the tools to do these tasks for almost no cost compared to hiring an entire team to carry out these tasks. On a similar note, there were barely any "AI ML developer and stimulator" job roles around in the past decade. Now, they are one of the most demanded and high-paying jobs in the world. Times have changed. The job market has changed. What is still the same? The inner side of the job, vis-a-vis, internal development and growth for employees. They are still judged on the same mental and social parameters. It also gets worse, not only are you required to drain out your brain using complex software and applications but also ensure whenever your manager looks up from his desk, you are drenched in work or whatever is it that just makes your manager happy.

But if overwork is the norm for Millennials, how does Gen Z approach career growth? Their perspective is starkly different. Unlike previous generations, their approach tends to be more nuanced, focusing not just on the outcome, but also on the process and the learning that comes with it. For them promotions are pivotal candies they receive every time they bring home a medal. This is just like other hard-working individuals, be it from any generation. But the distinction we need to discuss here is how we see and measure our performance vs our managers. For me, developing a new process to enhance efficiency, create output, or automate repetitive tasks would account for a majority of my performance review document as they demonstrate my skills and how well I understand the job at the same time my zeal to stand out and not just do what we are" asked to do". Along with these social attributes like maintaining harmony in the team and active participation in team-building activities would count for the remainder. What makes things complicated is when these "theoretical" and "official" parameters of performance measurement are mapped in correlation with the duration of your lunch break!

For someone working in cities like Delhi when the temperature is furiously rising and provided, we have the boon to be able to complete all our work whilst working comfortably from home, going to the office as a social stance does not only waste time due to commute and traffic but also takes a toll on your physical health. During these extreme weather conditions isn't it more important that the employees are able to fulfil their duties in a healthy environment or is it more important for our millennial managers to "urge" us to be in the office every day in lieu of enhanced productivity and easier communication, just so he can curate a detailed account of how many coffee breaks I took!

Even if we ignore the passive-aggressive and partially mean implications that take a toll on your mental health and lead you to self-doubt and stress, we cannot ignore the fact that these instances coherently link up to how your performance is measured. The next time your managers take up your performance review where you have rambled about effective communication and adherence to timelines, all they are going to think is- "There's no way they could've had effective communication with the team, they were barely ever in office" or "If they would've been in the office on most days, as suggested, I could've known about the work timelines the minute it got done. Communicating via mail/chat kills time." The point is that they would always choose the 2 minutes you save in communicating via chat vs in-person over the 45 minutes of commute you need to take every day. You are seldom obliged to screw your work schedule along with your personal commitments just because you happened to stumble upon a manager who feels more productive in an office setup. If we go back to our analogy about the journey these managers have had. Most of them have spent most of their lives in an in-office set up which has sort of made them used to this pattern. We, on the other hand, were on the brink of our careers when hybrid and work-from-home setups became as common as salt.

Given the influence of technology in the education system for Gen Z, they tend to be more technologically reliable and adaptable. This makes them fast learners especially when it comes to technology. With every company deadly focused on digitization and automation, such tech-savvy, fast learners can be a real asset to the team. However, these employees are subjected to work under millennial managers, who often forget the value technology is bringing to the table.

Some millennial managers believe that the gen z knows too much and they know that they know too much. Today, 20-year-olds are placed in top institutions with double-digit packages, a horrifying truth for the older generation. Today people have a much higher disposable income as well as numerous sources of income than people did a couple of decades ago. As technology grows, the salaries of people who know what to do and how to do increase exponentially. This happens irrespective of experience or seniority. At the end of the day, if you don't know how to do your job you are not really worth what you are paid. But is the reverse true as well? If you really know how to do your job, are you valued accordingly? Hand to heart, do you not know anyone who has been in this position? Who is toiling in hopes of being valued like they thought they would be? We all have either been there or know someone who has. All of this creates a disheartening juxtaposition with not being promoted or appreciated at the right time by the right manager

Beyond leadership, corporate culture plays a silent but powerful role in determining career progression. In traditional firms, networking, visibility, and "sticking to the process" hold as much weight as performance. But in modern, fast-paced companies, agility, upskilling, and adaptability matter more than tenure. This is why Gen Z thrives in startups, while millennials are often more comfortable in structured corporate environments.

As the corporate world continues to evolve, the definition of success is also shifting. Will tenure-based promotions remain the standard? Or will we see a shift where impact-driven work takes precedence over years of service? That remains an open question.

In essence, the corporate ladder would be a lot smoother if professionals adhered to standard performance metrics instead of personal judgments and innuendos. Keeping generational differences in mind is the right way to approach fair and harmonious performance feedback. But climbing the corporate ladder isn't just about how hard you work or how well you perform—it's also about how much of yourself you give to your job.

So, as we climb the corporate ladder, we must ask: Is success worth it if it comes at the cost of personal well-being? That's what we'll explore in the next chapter—Work-Life Balance: A Myth or a Necessity?

4.) Beyond 9 to 5

For Gen Z, work-life balance isn't just a buzzword; it's a fundamental approach to life and work. Unlike previous generations, who often accepted the blurred lines between personal time and professional commitments as the price of success, Gen Z is reshaping what it means to balance responsibilities. For them, work is a part of life, not the centre of it, and they're determined to create a future where this principle is universally respected. The heavy pressure of constant availability that has defined corporate culture in the past is seen by Gen Z as a form of corporate exertion—a strenuous demand that sacrifices personal well-being for professional gains. In response, they are challenging traditional structures, hoping to reclaim control over their time and mental space.

This outlook stems from the world they've grown up in—a world of relentless connectivity and constant change. They've witnessed their parents and older colleagues endure long hours, suffer burnout, and sacrifice personal joys for professional obligations. Many of them grew up hearing the phrase "work hard now, rest later," only to see the "later" never come. These experiences have significantly shaped their attitudes, instilling a deep conviction that life is too short to be spent solely on work. As we discussed earlier, corporate exertion has long been an accepted reality for previous generations. However, Gen Z is consciously pushing back, prioritizing efficiency in their careers over sheer endurance. They're wary of falling into a cycle of exhaustion that their predecessors endured, and they want a more sustainable approach to their careers.

Millennial managers, in their roles as leaders and bridge-builders within organizations, approach work-life balance with a perspective shaped by unique challenges and experiences. Unlike the Gen Z workforce, whose career trajectories began in a world increasingly aware of the need for balance, millennials grew up in an era where ambition often demanded sacrifice, and success was synonymous with relentless hustle. As the first generation to straddle the worlds of analog and digital, they have navigated an unprecedented pace of change, adapting to new technologies, evolving industries, and shifting societal expectations. Their approach to personal and professional alignment is nuanced, reflective of their journey through economic upheavals, rapid technological advancements, and now, the responsibility of leading teams in a transformed corporate sphere. Despite this awareness, however, many millennial managers still wrestle with the very exhaustion that Gen Z actively seeks to avoid.

Gen Z's stance on work-life harmony is rooted in their ability to adapt to technology and use it to streamline their tasks. Unlike older generations who often equate long hours with dedication, they believe in working smarter, not harder. They value efficiency and productivity over the number of hours clocked at a desk. To them, success is not about being the first one in and the last one out of the office but about achieving goals effectively while leaving time for personal pursuits. This shift in how work is perceived is directly linked to the desire to avoid corporate exhaustion, which occurs when employees feel they must be constantly engaged to prove their value. Gen Z is advocating for a system that prioritizes results over raw input, which would significantly reduce the mental and physical toll many workers face.

This generation is particularly drawn to flexibility in work arrangements. Whether it's remote work, hybrid models, or flexible hours, Gen Z sees these options not as perks but as basic expectations. They understand that their best work comes when they have the freedom to structure their day according to their energy levels and personal commitments. They reject the rigidity of traditional 9-to-5 schedules, arguing that the quality of work should take precedence over the quantity of hours worked. The traditional office-based model often leads to corporate exhaustion, where employees are expected to perform at high levels without considering the impact on their mental or emotional health. Gen Z seeks to break free from this by promoting flexible work practices that allow employees to recharge and avoid burnout.

While, for many millennial managers, the concept of balance is a hard-earned realization rather than an innate priority. Their early professional lives were dominated by the hustle culture that glorified long hours and a willingness to do whatever it took to climb the corporate ladder. Success, as defined during their formative years, was rooted in visible productivity—an image of dedication that often came at the expense of personal well-being. They entered the workforce during a time of significant financial instability, with the 2008 global recession casting a long shadow over their career prospects. Layoffs, stagnant wages, and fierce competition for jobs pushed them to prove their worth through sheer effort, leaving little room for balance. However, the exhaustion that accompanied this culture eventually took its toll, resulting in burnout for many who now hold managerial roles. Many millennial managers are thus faced with a paradox: they understand the dangers of corporate exertion but often feel compelled to withhold the very practices that caused it in the first place.

Gen Z's emphasis on balance extends beyond just scheduling. Gen Z is vocal about the importance of mental health and well-being in the workplace. They are unafraid to speak up when they feel overwhelmed or unsupported, and they expect their employers to take these concerns seriously. For them, a healthy work-life equation isn't just about time management; it's about creating a culture where employees feel valued and respected. They expect companies to provide resources such as mental health days, access to therapy, and policies that discourage overwork. These practices aim to prevent corporate exhaustion, where the mental load becomes unbearable, leading to stress, anxiety, and eventual burnout. By addressing these issues directly, Gen Z is paving the way for a healthier corporate environment.

This approach often challenges traditional workplace norms. Older generations, including the millennial managers, largely grew up with the mindset that work should always come first, and sometimes perceive Gen Z's priorities as entitlement. However, it's not about being entitled; it's about being intentional. Gen Z has seen firsthand the consequences of a life consumed by work, and they're determined not to follow that path. Many of them have witnessed the toll that overwork has taken on their families, friends, and colleagues, leading to corporate exhaustion in the form of burnout, mental health crises, and strained personal relationships. They're committed to finding a more balanced approach.

One of the key ways Gen Z maintains a work-life balance is by setting clear boundaries. They understand the importance of protecting their personal time and are unafraid to say no to tasks that encroach on it. For them, boundaries are not about shirking responsibility but about ensuring sustainability in their work. This practice often surprises older colleagues who may view such assertiveness as audacious, but Gen Z sees it as essential for long-term productivity and satisfaction. Establishing these boundaries is a direct countermeasure against such burnout, ensuring that they don't overextend themselves in pursuit of success.

Technology has played a significant role in shaping their perspectives. Growing up in a digitally connected world, they've witnessed the pros and cons of being "always on." While they leverage technology to stay efficient and connected, they are also keenly aware of the need to unplug and recharge. They prioritize digital boundaries, such as turning off notifications outside of work hours or taking regular breaks from screens, to ensure they don't become overwhelmed. This digital detox is another strategy to avoid the trap of corporate exhaustion, where constant connectivity can lead to burnout and a blurring of lines between work and personal life.

Gen Z also places a strong emphasis on aligning their work with their values. They are less likely to tolerate toxic workplace cultures or companies that don't prioritize inclusivity, diversity, and sustainability. For them, setting life and work harmony isn't just about having some personal time after their 9 to 5 jobs; it's about working in an environment that respects their principles. They seek out roles and organizations that allow them to make a meaningful impact without compromising their personal lives. This desire for meaningful work often correlates with avoiding burnout, as they know that their emotional and mental energy should be invested in projects and causes, they care about, rather than in environments that drain them.

This generational mindset is transforming the workplace in many ways. Companies are beginning to recognize that accommodating Gen Z's expectations isn't just a matter of retention—it's a matter of staying relevant. Organizations that fail to adapt risk losing out on a talented and innovative workforce. As a result, many companies are reevaluating their policies, offering greater flexibility, and investing in employee well-being initiatives. However, this transformation is not without its challenges. Many millennial managers, caught between the traditional ways of working and the new demands of Gen Z, are struggling to balance their personal and professional commitments, often feeling the weight of corporate exertion themselves.

Despite their progressive stance, Gen Z's pursuit of work-life balance isn't without challenges. They often face resistance from older colleagues and managers who view their approach as unrealistic or incompatible with business goals. Bridging this gap requires open communication and mutual understanding. It's essential for organizations to promote an environment where different generational perspectives are respected and integrated. However, millennial managers, while largely supportive of these changes, often find themselves stuck in a difficult position: they understand the need for balance, but they still feel the pressure to uphold the traditional models of work that lead to corporate exhaustion. This generational divide creates tension, as millennial managers attempt to guide teams toward a balanced approach while simultaneously managing their own exhaustion.

As millennials step into managerial roles, millennial leaders carry the weight of those early career pressures while facing a new reality: they are responsible not only for their own growth but also for the well-being and development of their teams. This dual responsibility forces them to reevaluate their relationship with work and find ways to balance their personal lives with their professional commitments. Unlike earlier generations, who often adhered to rigid hierarchies and traditional definitions of leadership, millennial managers tend to be more empathetic and open to new ideas. They understand the value of creating supportive work environments, but they also grapple with their own ingrained habits of overwork and self-sacrifice. This struggle to find balance while managing expectations often leads to corporate exertion, as millennial managers feel compelled to continuously perform at high levels while supporting their teams.

For Gen Z, this is not a one-size-fits-all concept. They recognize that everyone has unique needs and preferences, and they advocate for a personalized approach. They believe that employees should have the autonomy to define what balance looks like for them and the flexibility to achieve it. This mindset represents a significant departure from the rigid structures of the past, offering a glimpse into a future where work is truly integrated into life rather than dominating it. However, while Gen Z is focused on avoiding corporate exertion, millennial managers are often caught in the middle, trying to model balance while navigating the expectations and pressures that come with leadership roles.

The impact of Gen Z's perspective on career-life synergy extends beyond individual workplaces. It's sparking broader conversations about the nature of work and its role in our lives. By challenging outdated norms and advocating for change, Gen Z is paving the way for a more humane and inclusive future of work. They are reminding us that work should enhance our lives, not consume them, and that success is ultimately measured by the quality of life we lead.

However, for millennial managers, this transition can be difficult. They are still feeling the aftereffects of years spent in corporate environments that prized exertion overbalance. They recognize the need for change, but the path to achieving it remains fraught with challenges.

What sets millennial managers apart is their ability to adapt and learn. Many of them have seen the consequences of burnout firsthand, either in their own lives or in the lives of their peers. These experiences have made them more attuned to the importance of mental health and the need for boundaries between work and personal life. However, this awareness does not always translate into action. The deeply ingrained culture of overachievement can make it difficult for them to model the very balance they wish to promote. It's not uncommon for millennial managers to encourage their teams to take breaks and prioritize well-being while simultaneously struggling to disconnect themselves. The result is a constant tug-of-war between promoting well-being and enduring the exhaustion that corporate jobs demand.

Parenthood is another factor that influences how millennial managers reckon the work-life equation. Many are raising young families while navigating demanding careers, a combination that requires constant juggling and prioritization. This dual role has made them advocates for workplace policies that support flexibility and caregiving, such as parental leave, remote work options, and flexible schedules. Their lived experiences often drive them to push for changes that benefit not only themselves but also their teams, creating workplaces that are more accommodating and inclusive. However, balancing these responsibilities can be challenging, leading to an ongoing struggle with corporate exhaustion.

At the same time, millennial managers face the challenge of managing multigenerational teams with differing expectations. They often find themselves mediating between the traditional work ethic of older employees and the boundary-focused approach of Gen Z. This dynamic requires a delicate balance of understanding and negotiation, as they strive to create harmony while ensuring productivity. Millennial managers recognize the value of embracing diverse perspectives, but they also feel the pressure of meeting organizational goals in a way that satisfies everyone involved. The result is often a sense of exhaustion, as millennial managers are pushed to meet both their own expectations and those of their teams, sometimes at the cost of their well-being. But as Gen Z prioritizes balance, another pressing question arises—what does work truly mean to them? If they refuse to let it consume their identity, then what role does work play in their aspirations and self-worth?

In the next chapter, we'll explore whether work is just a means to an end or still holds deeper significance in their ambitions.

5.) More than Money....

Money has always been a fascinating lens through which we can observe societal values and individual priorities. For generations, the concept of financial success has been a driving force, shaping career choices, lifestyle aspirations, and even relationships. But as we examine the contrast between Gen Z and Millennials, it becomes evident that their perspectives on money differ significantly, shaped by the vastly different worlds they grew up in. These differences, born out of distinct economic realities, technological advancements, and cultural narratives, provide compelling insights into how money is perceived, managed, and valued by each generation.

Millennials, often referred to as the "generation of delayed gratification," were raised in a world where financial success was tied to hard work, education, and patience. Many of them grew up during an era of relative economic stability in the 1990s but were quickly jolted into adulthood by the global financial crisis of 2008. This formative experience left an indelible mark on their financial outlook. For most Millennials, money became synonymous with security, and their financial goals often revolved around stability—buying a house, saving for retirement, and achieving debt-free living.

This focus on financial security isn't surprising when we consider the events that shaped their early careers. As Millennials entered the workforce, they encountered a job market marred by layoffs, stagnant wages, and fierce competition. Many struggled to find stable employment or were forced to accept lower-paying jobs The crushing burden of student loans only compounded the issue, leaving Millennials wary of risk and cautious with their finances.

Their cautious approach to money often translates into meticulous budgeting and a preference for experiences over material possessions. Millennials popularized trends like minimalist living and the "sharing economy," valuing access over ownership. Services like Airbnb and Uber became staples for Millennials, reflecting their pragmatic approach to spending.

In contrast, Gen Z's relationship with money has been shaped by an entirely different set of circumstances. Born into a world of rapid technological advancement and unprecedented access to information, Gen Z has grown up with a level of financial awareness that far exceeds that of previous generations at their age. While Millennials often learn about personal finance through trial and error, Gen Z has had access to financial education through YouTube videos, TikTok influencers, and apps that gamify budgeting and investing. This generation doesn't just understand money—they expect to wield it wisely from a young age.

Gen Z's approach to money is pragmatic yet ambitious. They've seen the struggles of Millennials—crippling student loans, the fallout of the housing crisis, and the pressure to conform to traditional financial milestones—and they've taken these lessons to heart. Unlike Millennials, who often entered adulthood with an "earn, save, and spend" mentality, Gen Z is focused on diversification and long-term growth. They are more likely to invest in stocks, cryptocurrencies, and other assets at a younger age, leveraging technology to make informed financial decisions.

However, this pragmatic approach doesn't mean Gen Z is immune to financial pressures. The rising cost of living, coupled with economic instability from events like the COVID-19 pandemic, has made financial independence a challenging goal for many. Yet, instead of being deterred, Gen Z has developed a resilience that allows them to adapt quickly. Whether it's turning a side hustle into a full-time job or leveraging social media to build a personal brand, they're redefining what financial success looks like in the modern age.

The cultural narratives surrounding money have also evolved between the two generations. For Millennials, money talk was often taboo, confined to private conversations or professional settings. They were taught to avoid discussing salaries or financial struggles, perpetuating a culture of secrecy that often-hindered collective growth. Gen Z, on the other hand, is breaking down these barriers. They are more open about their earnings, investments, and financial goals, cultivating a culture of transparency that encourages dialogue and learning. This openness has the potential to dismantle systemic inequities, as it empowers individuals to negotiate better salaries and advocate for fair compensation.

Another critical difference lies in how each generation views the role of money in their lives. For many Millennials, money is a means to an end—a tool for achieving stability and fulfilling responsibilities. Gen Z, however, sees money as a way to enhance their quality of life and align their work with their passions. This distinction is evident in their career choices; Gen Z is more likely to prioritize job satisfaction and meaningful engagement over a high salary, reflecting a desire to integrate their personal values with their professional lives.

The priorities of Gen Z extend far beyond financial gain. They place immense value on mental health and workplace benefits that cater to holistic well-being. For Gen Z, an ideal job is one that doesn't merely pay the bills but also provides an environment where employees feel seen, heard, and valued. Inclusivity, for them, is a fundamental principle rather than a corporate buzzword. They expect companies to go beyond tokenism and actively create environments where diversity of thought, background, and experience is celebrated and harnessed for innovation.

The digital landscape has also played a pivotal role in shaping these perceptions. Millennials witnessed the rise of e-commerce and online banking, but Gen Z has grown up with online transfers, UPI, and cryptocurrencies. The ease and immediacy of digital transactions have made them more comfortable with managing money online, but it has also created a culture of instant gratification that can sometimes conflict with long-term financial planning. However, their tech-savviness enables them to leverage tools like budgeting apps and investment platforms, helping them strike a balance between immediate desires and future goals.

Gen Z advocates for workplaces that implement tangible policies ensuring diverse representation at all levels of the organization, from entry-level positions to executive leadership. They seek companies that prioritize equitable hiring practices, offer comprehensive bias training, and create safe spaces for underrepresented groups. Diversity is not just a checkbox for this generation; it is a dynamic force that drives creativity and productivity within a thriving corporate culture.

Moreover, Gen Z expects organizations to actively address systemic inequalities through transparent practices and accountability. This includes setting measurable diversity goals and regularly reporting progress to employees and stakeholders. They appreciate companies that recognize intersectionality—acknowledging that individuals' identities are multifaceted and that true inclusivity requires understanding and addressing overlapping forms of discrimination. Such efforts demonstrate a commitment to genuine progress and resonate deeply with Gen Z's values.

Inclusivity also extends to corporate policies that accommodate diverse needs, such as flexible work arrangements, inclusive parental leave policies, and benefits that cater to various family structures. Gen Z values workplaces that provide accessibility for individuals with disabilities and ensure all employees have the tools and resources to thrive. They view inclusivity not as an isolated effort but as an integral aspect of a supportive and equitable workplace culture. Gen Z doesn't see inclusivity as just another corporate PR move or hollow attempt at "fake positivity." To them, it's about truly embracing diversity and building workplaces where authenticity and meaningful change take centre stage.

In essence, inclusivity for Gen Z is about building an organizational culture that respects, values, and uplifts everyone. They are drawn to companies that take proactive steps to ensure every voice is heard, every perspective is considered, and every individual feels empowered to contribute their best work. This relentless focus on inclusivity is not just a preference but a defining characteristic of how Gen Z reimagines the workplace of the future.

Furthermore, mental health has emerged as a non-negotiable aspect of workplace satisfaction for Gen Z. They are vocal about the need for comprehensive mental health resources, ranging from access to therapy and wellness programs to enabling a culture where employees feel safe discussing their challenges without fear of stigma or reprisal. Flexible schedules, mental health days, and workplace initiatives promoting emotional well-being are no longer considered perks for this generation; they are baseline expectations that reflect a larger cultural shift.

This insistence on prioritizing mental health is not without context. Gen Z's openness about mental health stands in stark contrast to the experiences of Millennials, who often faced significant stigma surrounding the topic. For many Millennials, mental health struggles were either ignored or dismissed as personal weaknesses. Growing up during a time when seeking professional help was often stigmatized, Millennials learned to push through challenges silently, prioritizing work over their well-being. This societal attitude led to a normalization of burnout and chronic stress, leaving many Millennials ill-equipped to recognize or address their mental health needs.

Gen Z, however, has rejected these outdated notions. They have grown up in an era where mental health conversations are more visible and widely accepted, thanks to social media advocacy and increasing public discourse. They view mental health as an integral part of overall well-being and demand that employers do the same. Gen Z's willingness to prioritize their mental health—even at the cost of traditional corporate expectations—is reshaping workplace norms. They advocate for organizations to adopt a more compassionate and human-cantered approach to employee care, ensuring that mental health support is embedded in the workplace culture rather than being treated as an afterthought.

This generational divergence also highlights an important opportunity for collaboration. By addressing the stigma that hindered Millennials and embracing the proactive stance of Gen Z, organizations can create environments where mental health is openly discussed and effectively supported. For Millennials, this can mean unlearning harmful coping mechanisms and adopting healthier approaches to work-life integration. For Gen Z, it reinforces their belief that workplaces can and should be spaces that prioritize holistic well-being.

In addition to mental health, Gen Z places a strong emphasis on physical well-being. Fitness and health-related benefits have become pivotal in attracting and retaining Gen Z talent. Gym memberships, wellness stipends, and access to fitness facilities are perks that resonate deeply with this generation. They view physical health as integral to their overall productivity and quality of life, and they expect their workplaces to support this ethos. Initiatives that encourage active lifestyles, such as team fitness challenges or subsidized wellness programs, are particularly appealing to this cohort.

The emphasis on diversity and equity also translates into Gen Z's expectations for their workplace's broader social responsibilities. They want to work for organizations that align with their values, particularly in areas such as environmental sustainability, social justice, and ethical practices. Companies that demonstrate a commitment to these principles—through tangible actions rather than performative statements—are more likely to attract and retain Gen Z employees. For this generation, the alignment between personal and corporate values is a significant factor in job satisfaction and loyalty.

Gen Z's demand for an exhaustive approach to workplace benefits is reshaping traditional compensation structures. While Millennials prioritized stability through retirement plans and long-term financial security, Gen Z seeks a more immediate and diverse range of benefits. This includes everything from student loan repayment assistance to opportunities for professional development and skills training. They value companies that invest in their growth, not just as employees but as individuals with evolving aspirations.

Gen Z's approach to money and work is not just a reflection of their individual preferences but also of the evolving societal sphere. Their emphasis on transparency and well-being signals a shift in workplace dynamics that organizations must adapt to. For instance, the rise of social enterprises, which balance profit with purpose, aligns closely with Gen Z's ideals. These businesses are not just profitable but also socially and environmentally conscious, attracting a generation that values meaningful contributions over mere financial gain.

For instance, In India, Amul, founded in 1946, operates as one of India's largest dairy cooperatives, empowering millions of dairy farmers by providing fair prices and stable incomes, thereby significantly improving rural economies. Amul fosters a positive organizational culture through fair hiring practices, comprehensive employee programs, and performance management initiatives. The company emphasizes innovation and teamwork, ensuring that employees feel motivated and satisfied. Amul also recognizes employee contributions by organizing annual events and offering rewards such as cars, cash prizes, and family trips to high achievers. These efforts contribute to a supportive work environment, which is reflected in employee reviews. On Glassdoor, Amul holds an overall rating of 4.1 out of 5, with 79% of employees indicating they would recommend the company to a friend.

Another example is Greyston Bakery, established in 1982 in Yonkers, New York. Greyston employs an "Open Hiring" policy, offering jobs to individuals regardless of their background or work history. This inclusive approach has led to a 69% employee retention rate after 90 days. The bakery reinvests its profits into community programs like affordable housing and childcare, demonstrating a successful balance between financial performance and social responsibility.

These businesses exemplify how profitability can coexist with social responsibility and high employee retention, resonating with a generation that values meaningful contributions over mere financial gain.

Furthermore, Gen Z's focus on personal and professional growth has led to a greater demand for mentorship and learning opportunities. They are not content with stagnant roles and expect employers to provide continuous development options. Companies that fail to offer such opportunities risk losing their top talent to competitors who understand the value of investing in their workforce's future.

As Gen Z continues to enter the workforce in greater numbers, their expectations will undoubtedly influence organizational strategies. Companies that adapt by prioritizing holistic benefits, promoting an inclusive culture, and embracing flexibility will be better positioned to attract and retain this dynamic generation. On the other hand, organizations that cling to outdated practices risk becoming irrelevant in an increasingly competitive talent market.

While both generations face unique financial challenges, their differing approaches highlight a broader societal shift. Millennials, shaped by adversity and cautious optimism, have paved the way for a more flexible and experience-driven financial culture. Gen Z, with their entrepreneurial mindset and digital savviness, is pushing the boundaries further, redefining traditional notions of success and creating new opportunities for financial empowerment. This redefinition extends to the workplace, where Gen Z's holistic approach to well-being and inclusivity is setting new standards for what employees can and should expect from their employers.

Ultimately, the contrasting philosophies of these two generations underscore the importance of understanding and adapting to the evolving nature of work and money. By learning from each other's experiences and perspectives, Millennials and Gen Z can facilitate a more inclusive and innovative approach to financial well-being—one that values not just stability but also growth, adaptability, and a shared commitment to a better future. Organizations that recognize and embrace these shifts will not only attract top talent but also cultivate a workforce that thrives on shared values and mutual respect. This evolution in workplace culture and priorities is more than a trend; it is a necessary adaptation to the demands of a new generation shaping the future of work.

The Entrepreneurial Spirit

The entrepreneurial drive among Gen Z extends far beyond a simple preference for self-employment or business ownership—it represents a shift in how they view work as a means of self-expression, financial independence, and problem-solving. For Gen Z, entrepreneurship is not just about financial gain; it is a way to create value, address societal issues, and carve out a unique identity in a competitive world. This generation's comfort with digital tools and global connectivity has redefined the traditional barriers to entry, making business ventures more accessible than ever before.

Gen Z entrepreneurs often approach business with a tech-first mentality, leveraging platforms like Shopify, Substack, or Patreon to monetize their ideas quickly. They frequently experiment with diverse revenue streams, such as e-commerce stores, content creation, digital art, and software development. Their willingness to embrace emerging trends like the creator economy, blockchain technology, and Web3 highlights their adaptability and eagerness to be at the forefront of innovation. They prioritize agility and scalability in their ventures, focusing on solutions that can grow rapidly with minimal resources.

Additionally, the entrepreneurial mindset in this generation is deeply tied to their values. Gen Z entrepreneurs are more likely to align their business models with personal beliefs, including sustainability, ethical practices, and social impact. This approach not only attracts like-minded consumers but also creates a sense of fulfilment that goes beyond monetary success. Education and skill development also play a pivotal role in their entrepreneurial journey. Unlike previous generations, who may have relied on formal education as the primary path to career success, Gen Z turns to online courses, workshops, and self-paced learning platforms to acquire the skills they need. They actively seek out knowledge on coding, marketing, design, and business strategy, often learning from successful entrepreneurs who share their insights on social media or YouTube.

One distinguishing characteristic is their use of social media as both a tool for marketing and a platform for community building. Platforms like Instagram, TikTok, and LinkedIn allow Gen Z entrepreneurs to reach global audiences with minimal upfront investment. They use these spaces not just to promote their products or services but also to connect directly with their audience, building trust and authenticity.

For example, Griffin Haddrill, co-founder of VRTCL, has leveraged TikTok to create viral marketing campaigns for artists like Justin Bieber. By engaging directly with users and adapting to real-time feedback, he has built a strong community around the brands he represents, demonstrating the power of social media in modern entrepreneurship. This direct engagement enables Gen Z entrepreneurs to refine their offerings in real time, adapting quickly to consumer feedback.

Lastly, the entrepreneurial energy of Gen Z is fuelled by their readiness to embrace failure as a stepping stone to success. They understand that risk-taking is an inherent part of building something new, and they are often willing to pivot their ideas or start over entirely when faced with setbacks. This resilience, coupled with their resourcefulness and drive, positions them as a generation ready to redefine traditional notions of business and work.

While Gen Z's entrepreneurial tendencies are shaped by technological advancements and societal shifts, Millennials laid much of the groundwork for this mindset. Millennials entered adulthood during a time when traditional career paths were beginning to falter. The 2008 financial crisis left many Millennials disillusioned with the corporate world, pushing them to explore self-employment and innovation as viable alternatives. For Millennials, entrepreneurship was often born out of necessity rather than choice—a way to regain control in an uncertain economic environment.

Unlike Gen Z, whose entrepreneurial journey is deeply intertwined with digital tools from the start, Millennials had to adapt as these technologies emerged. Platforms like Facebook and YouTube were in their infancy when Millennials began exploring business ventures, and they learned to harness these tools as they evolved. Many of the influencers, vloggers, and e-commerce pioneers we see today are Millennials who paved the way for digital entrepreneurship, transforming hobbies and passions into full-fledged businesses.

The Millennial approach to entrepreneurship often emphasizes long-term impact and stability, reflecting their broader outlook on financial security. Many Millennials focus on building businesses that can provide consistent income while aligning with their interests and values. They are also more likely to venture into industries that require significant expertise or credentials, such as consulting, healthcare, or education, using their knowledge and skills to create niche opportunities.

However, Millennial entrepreneurs also face unique challenges, including balancing the demands of starting a business with responsibilities such as student debt, raising families, or saving for the future. This juggling act has instilled a strong sense of resilience and resourcefulness, qualities that continue to define Millennial entrepreneurship.

In essence, while Gen Z may be redefining what entrepreneurship looks like in a hyper-connected world, Millennials were the architects of many foundational shifts in modern business. Together, these generations are driving a new wave of innovation, creativity, and purpose-driven enterprise that is shaping the future of work and commerce.

6.) Redefining Dream Jobs

In the past, securing a prestigious corporate job was the pinnacle of success. It was the culmination of years of education, internships, and networking. Graduates would proudly walk into their first office job, anticipating the rewards of their hard work: the respect of colleagues, the sense of accomplishment, and the financial security that came with it. Corporate careers were not just about earning a pay check; they were the foundation for a comfortable life and, in many ways, the key to future opportunities. Many aspired to work for large corporations, driven by the prospect of steady promotions, lucrative benefits, and the promise of stability.

But the world has changed. The allure of climbing the corporate ladder seems to be fading. Over the past decade, we've witnessed a shift—a growing disillusionment with corporate structures, long hours, and hierarchical office environments. Today, many of the younger generation, particularly Gen Z, are rethinking the corporate dream. They're questioning the value of traditional office jobs and opting to leave behind the stability they once offered. This shift is no longer just a trend; it's become a defining movement in the workplace. More and more people are walking away from their corporate roles in search of more fulfilling and flexible career options.

What happened to those once prestigious corporate jobs that seemed to fulfil every professional wish? After all the hardships you face in college to secure the best placement, followed by dedicating yourself entirely to earning that long-awaited promotion, and then exhausting all your contacts to land the next switch, many are now finding themselves chasing something different—something that truly resonates with their desires and needs. We chase happiness, we chase the rewards of our efforts, and we chase the lifestyle. Ultimately, we chase the money. But, more importantly, we also want to chase our passions and aspirations outside of the confines of a corporate environment.

What if I told you that you can achieve all of this—career success, personal fulfilment, and financial security—without working 12-hour days, sacrificing weekends, and toiling away for someone else's benefit? What if you could have it all while maintaining a work-life balance, enjoying a life outside work, and even pursuing your passions? Just a few years ago, this might have sounded too good to be true. Today, however, it is a reality. Careers in content creation, marketing, and social media management, or the flexibility offered by freelancing and part-time work, now offer dependable and high-income streams. So, why are so many Gen Z employees quitting their well-paying corporate jobs to pursue these alternative paths? Why are they choosing liberal fields over traditional corporate careers? The simplest answer is: why not? But there's much more to unpack here.

The times have changed, and so have perspectives about work and career paths. A few decades ago, following your passion was a dream chased by a few brave individuals while being an engineer, followed by an MNC job was the epitome of success and bought bragging rights for the parents. For most people, the corporate world offered stability and security—two pillars that eliminated uncertainty from daily life. It promised a dependable pay check, a guarantee of food on the table, rent paid, and the occasional luxury. This sense of security motivated generations to work diligently within corporate structures, building savings and providing better opportunities for their children. These children, now Gen Z, grew up with exposure to a wider world, enabled by their parents' financial stability and access to private education, extracurricular training, and opportunities to explore their passions. Academic education was no longer a boundary; career options seemed limitless. Yet, societal norms still dictated acceptable career choices. While time has begun to fill this gap, technology has been the real catalyst in transforming career dynamics.

Technology has reshaped both corporate and non-corporate careers. Companies now aspire to be technologically advanced, creating high-paying jobs in tech. At the same time, the internet has democratized access to opportunities. Rural and urban areas alike are now connected, with mobile phones and social media enabling individuals to reach global audiences. Technology has made mainstream education and livelihoods accessible to many. The COVID-19 pandemic further accelerated this shift. It instilled a sense of "life is too short," prompting people to take leaps of faith. The rise of digital careers—from social media marketing to content creation—was almost overwhelming. Influencers and creators began earning substantial incomes, proving that passion and flexibility could coexist with financial success. As societal acceptance grew, these careers transitioned from being viewed as liberal and low-paying to lucrative and aspirational. The result? A mass exodus from traditional corporate jobs.

Gen Z, more than the millennials or any previous generation, is wholeheartedly embracing the gig economy and freelancing as transformative career paths. Unlike the traditional 9-to-5 job, which often ties individuals to a rigid schedule and a single employer, the gig economy provides unparalleled freedom and adaptability. For many young professionals, freelancing isn't just a fallback option; it isn't just something you do along with your job to earn some extra money, it has become a strategic choice to design careers around their passions and lifestyles. Platforms like Fiverr, Upwork, and TaskRabbit have revolutionized access to work opportunities, enabling individuals to showcase their skills to global clients without geographical constraints.

This ecosystem thrives on flexibility. Freelancers can define their schedules, choose projects that align with their interests, and avoid the monotony of repetitive tasks. Gen Z values this level of autonomy as it allows them to integrate personal goals with professional aspirations. Many young professionals view freelancing as a platform to diversify their skill sets while avoiding the burnout often associated with traditional office jobs. The ability to dictate workload and work environment empowers individuals to maintain a healthier work-life balance while maximizing productivity.

Furthermore, the gig economy has cultivated a space for creativity and innovation. For instance, content creators on YouTube or TikTok use these platforms to build personal brands and connect directly with audiences. Influencers and streamers leverage tools like Patreon and Twitch subscriptions to create steady revenue streams while engaging with their followers in meaningful ways. Photographers, designers, and even educators have embraced digital marketplaces such as Etsy and Teachable, offering unique products and courses that cater to niche audiences. These platforms not only democratize opportunities but also reward individuality, enabling freelancers to stand out by highlighting their distinct talents.

The transition to freelancing is also reshaping the financial dynamics for Gen Z. Many have recognized that relying solely on traditional employment is no longer sustainable in a rapidly changing economic environment. Instead, they are creating multiple revenue streams to ensure financial stability and growth. For example, a graphic designer might balance client commissions with earnings from selling digital assets on creative marketplaces. Similarly, a writer could combine income from freelance projects, self-published e-books, and paid subscriptions on platforms like Substack. This diversification allows professionals to weather economic uncertainties while exploring various avenues for financial success.

At the heart of this shift is the accessibility of digital tools and platforms that make freelancing and multi-revenue strategies feasible for anyone with an internet connection. Skill-sharing platforms like Coursera and Skillshare enable Gen Z to continually enhance their expertise, often at a fraction of the cost of traditional education. By leveraging these resources, many freelancers can adapt to industry trends and offer cutting-edge services that set them apart in competitive markets. The result is a workforce that is not only agile but also exceptionally well-equipped to navigate the demands of a dynamic economy.

Moreover, this diversified approach to income generation goes beyond financial benefits. It provides a sense of fulfilment and ownership that is often lacking in conventional roles. Gen Z professionals are finding purpose in crafting careers that align with their values, whether it involves championing social causes, promoting sustainability, or pursuing creative ambitions. By combining various income streams, they are building lives that reflect their multifaceted identities, proving that work can be both profitable and meaningful.

The gig economy offers unparalleled flexibility and autonomy, allowing individuals to balance their professional and personal lives more effectively. Freelancers and independent contractors can choose their clients, set their rates, and define their schedules. This level of control is particularly appealing to Gen Z, who value work-life integration and the freedom to pursue diverse interests. The gig economy also aligns with their entrepreneurial spirit. Many young professionals see freelancing not as a stopgap but as a long-term career choice, offering both financial independence and creative fulfilment.

Social media has played a crucial role in normalizing these alternative career paths. Platforms like TikTok and Instagram have turned everyday individuals into influencers with significant earning potential. Gen Z has grown up witnessing peers achieve success through content creation, instilling a belief that traditional career trajectories are no longer the only route to financial stability. This visibility has inspired a wave of digital entrepreneurs who are unafraid to explore unconventional paths.

However, the gig economy is not without its challenges. Unlike traditional corporate roles, freelancers often lack access to benefits such as health insurance, retirement plans, and paid leave. The unpredictability of income can also be a significant drawback. Yet, Gen Z's resourcefulness and adaptability enable them to navigate these challenges effectively. Many freelancers diversify their income streams to mitigate financial risks, combining multiple gigs or projects to create a stable and sustainable livelihood.

This shift towards alternative career paths reflects a broader cultural transformation. Gen Z's rejection of traditional corporate norms is not just about dissatisfaction with office life; it's about redefining success on their terms. They prioritize purpose, flexibility, and authenticity over prestige and hierarchy. This mindset is reshaping the professional environment, compelling organizations to rethink their value propositions and adapt to the changing expectations of the workforce.

The gig economy also offers an avenue for skill enhancement and career exploration. Many individuals use freelancing as a platform to experiment with different industries and roles, honing their expertise in diverse areas. For instance, a freelance graphic designer might simultaneously explore roles in digital marketing or product design, broadening their skill set and increasing their marketability. This approach allows Gen Z professionals to remain agile in an ever-changing job market, equipping them with the tools needed to adapt to future demands.

Additionally, the concept of financial diversification has gained traction among Gen Z professionals. The idea of relying on a single source of income seems outdated in a world where economic uncertainties are the norm. Instead, Gen Z is embracing the notion of multiple revenue streams, combining traditional jobs with side hustles, investments, and entrepreneurial ventures. This diversified approach not only provides financial security but also enables individuals to explore their passions without being tethered to a single career path. Platforms like Etsy, Shopify, and Substack offer countless opportunities for young professionals to monetize their hobbies and creative pursuits.

Digital platforms have also democratized education, enabling individuals to acquire new skills on their own terms. Online courses, webinars, and tutorials have made it easier than ever to learn marketable skills, from coding and graphic design to video editing and data analysis. This accessibility has empowered Gen Z to take charge of their professional development, bypassing traditional gatekeepers like universities and certification boards. By leveraging these resources, many young professionals are creating careers that align with their unique interests and talents.

As we look to the future, it's clear that the gig economy and alternative careers will continue to gain traction. Gen Z is leading this charge, proving that financial security and personal fulfilment are not mutually exclusive. By embracing technology, leveraging digital platforms, and prioritizing their passions, they are redefining what it means to build a successful career. In doing so, they are not just adapting to a changing world; they are actively shaping it, creating a professional environment that values individuality, creativity, and meaningful work.

7.) Way Ahead

Managers need to be trained on how to manage people, especially those from different generations. This is not just a suggestion—it's a necessity in today's multi-generational workplaces. As businesses evolve and grow, so do the needs and expectations of their employees, especially in organizations where multiple generations coexist. Managers who are tasked with leading such teams must be equipped with the right tools and strategies to navigate the complexities that arise when individuals from different generations, like Gen Z and millennials, work together.

In an era where generational differences are more prominent than ever, training managers to understand and manage these differences becomes a crucial component of organizational success. When individuals are promoted to managerial roles or hired directly into them, companies and human resource departments must take proactive steps to ensure they receive appropriate training. These training programs should not merely skim the surface but delve into the nuanced challenges of managing teams that include both Gen Z employees and millennial managers. It's essential for training to cover not only leadership techniques but also how to boost collaboration, encourage open communication, and address potential areas of conflict that might arise from differing generational values. Such programs can bridge the gap by emphasizing people-focused skills rather than task-oriented ones, a shift that reflects the evolving needs of the modern workforce.

For example, take the scenario of a millennial manager who struggles to connect with her younger team members. She might find herself frustrated by what she perceives as their lack of commitment when they choose not to respond to emails late at night, a behaviour she interprets as disengagement. However, after attending a comprehensive training program designed to address generational differences, she comes to realize that this behaviour is not a sign of laziness or lack of discipline. Instead, it's an embodiment of a value that is increasingly significant in today's workforce: the need to set healthy work-life boundaries. Gen Z, more than any generation before them, emphasizes mental well-being, and this includes establishing clear limits between work and personal life. The training helped the manager reframe her expectations and cultivate a more empathetic and open approach to leadership. This shift in mindset, while small, can have a multitude of effects on employee morale and team productivity.

Such instances highlight the importance of structured guidance in helping managers adjust to generational differences. Without the appropriate training, these differences can result in misunderstandings, reduced performance, and, at worst, workplace conflict. For example, another scenario might involve a millennial manager who expects his Gen Z employee to work long hours to meet tight deadlines. The Gen Z employee, however, might feel burnt out and unproductive after long periods of extended work hours, believing that working smarter is more efficient than simply working harder. This difference in work philosophy is an excellent opportunity for both parties to engage in a dialogue that can lead to better work practices, productivity, and understanding of each other's perspectives.

On the other hand, younger employees also have responsibilities. Gen Z employees, while advocating for boundaries and work-life balance, must strive to communicate their needs clearly and constructively. It's essential for them to recognize that not all managers are resistant to change; some simply need time and guidance to adapt. For instance, a Gen Z employee once shared how she approached her manager about the need for more flexible work hours. Instead of framing it as a demand, she thoughtfully explained how this flexibility would boost her productivity and overall performance. Her manager, initially hesitant, came around after seeing the tangible results of this arrangement. This experience demonstrated how a respectful and collaborative approach to communication can facilitate positive change. It also underlined the importance of mutual respect: while managers must adapt to changing expectations, younger employees must also acknowledge that their managers might require guidance to understand the benefits of these changes.

The role of companies in bridging these generational gaps cannot be overstated. Beyond just offering training programs, organizations need to actively encourage an inclusive culture where both younger and older generations can work together harmoniously. One way to achieve this is by implementing mentorship programs that encourage mutual learning. Companies must look beyond traditional mentorship structures, where senior employees solely guide younger ones, and focus on reverse mentoring programs. In these programs, younger employees can teach older colleagues about new technologies and innovative ways of working. For example, a tech-savvy Gen Z analyst once helped her millennial manager streamline workflows using AI tools. The result? Both the manager and employee benefitted from increased efficiency, while the younger employee earned the manager's trust and appreciation. Reverse mentoring not only improves organizational efficiency but also facilitates mutual respect and understanding between different generations.

Corporate leaders also have a critical role to play in prioritizing mental health and work-life balance. These issues are particularly significant for younger employees, who value self-care and stress management as much as if not more than, the job itself. Companies should implement policies that normalize taking breaks and using mental health resources without any stigma. For example, one company introduced mandatory "no-meeting" days and flexible working hours, resulting in higher job satisfaction across all generations. By demonstrating that employee well-being is a priority, companies can build trust and loyalty among their workforce, creating a culture where people are encouraged to take care of their physical and mental health.

Incorporating Gen Z's culture and mindset into daily corporate routines is an essential step in bridging generational gaps. Many organizations are now adopting policies and strategies that resonate with Gen Z's values and expectations. These changes aim to create a more inclusive and dynamic workplace that appeals to this younger generation while benefiting older generations as well. For example, unlimited leave policies have become more common as companies recognize that Gen Z values autonomy and trusts employees to manage their own time responsibly. A prime example of this is Netflix, which has successfully implemented an unlimited leave policy, trusting its employees to manage their time effectively while ensuring that work still gets done. This policy not only addresses Gen Z's demand for flexibility but also promotes a culture of mutual trust that resonates throughout the entire organization.

Similarly, external communications and marketing strategies have adapted to align with Gen Z's priorities. This generation is drawn to brands that demonstrate authenticity, inclusivity, and social responsibility. As a result, companies have increasingly hired younger employees to lead social media campaigns, provide insights into emerging trends, and help shape brand messaging. For instance, sportswear giant Nike frequently collaborates with Gen Z influencers to create campaigns that emphasize diversity and environmental awareness. This approach not only resonates with younger audiences but also ensures that internal corporate values align with external branding, creating a unified and appealing culture for employees and customers alike.

The evolving workplace dynamics, where companies rethink traditional hierarchies, have been particularly impactful in bridging generational divides. Many organizations are adopting flat organizational structures and encouraging cross-functional teams. This allows Gen Z employees to contribute ideas freely, without being constrained by rigid chains of command. For example, Google's "TGIF" program encourages open communication between employees and leadership, allowing individuals at all levels to share ideas and perspectives. Such initiatives help bridge generational divides by facilitating mutual understanding and respect between younger employees and seasoned managers.

As businesses reimagine how they provide learning and development opportunities, they are increasingly focusing on continuous growth—a value that resonates with Gen Z. Online courses, mentorship programs, and experiential learning opportunities are becoming key components of corporate training. Firms like Deloitte have introduced gamified learning platforms and microlearning modules that engage employees across all generations and provide opportunities for upskilling in a way that feels relevant and dynamic. This not only addresses the technological fluency of Gen Z but also allows employees from different generations to learn from one another, building a sense of camaraderie and cross-generational collaboration.

Creating workspaces that reflect Gen Z's emphasis on well-being and community is another crucial step. Modern office designs now prioritize natural lighting, collaborative zones, and wellness amenities like meditation rooms and fitness centres. For instance, Patagonia, renowned for its employee-first culture, integrates outdoor activities and sustainability efforts into its daily operations. These initiatives offer younger employees a sense of purpose, and when they see that the organization is committed to sustainability, they feel more connected to the company's mission. This alignment of values promotes a deeper connection to the workplace and enhances employee morale.

Drawing boundaries is another area where both managers and employees must collaborate. Managers should lead by example, demonstrating that it's okay to disconnect after work hours and take time off when needed. Simultaneously, Gen Z employees should understand that while boundaries are essential, collaboration and teamwork often require flexibility. Balancing individual needs with collective goals is crucial for any team's success.

As we've seen, the generational divide often stems from differing expectations about work. Millennials, for instance, grew up in a culture that valued the hustle. Their professional lives were shaped by a mindset that equated longer hours with greater dedication. Gen Z, however, questions this philosophy. They've grown up in a world where technology enables efficiency, and they see no reason to work longer hours when they can work smarter. This clash of philosophies presents an opportunity for mutual growth. Managers can learn to value efficiency and innovation, while younger employees can appreciate the experience and discipline that older generations bring to the table.

One real-world example comes from a tech company that implemented an innovative mentorship program. They paired younger employees with millennial managers to enable mutual understanding. The younger employees taught their managers about emerging technologies and trends, while the managers shared insights on navigating corporate politics and long-term career planning. This program not only bridged the generational gap but also created a collaborative culture that benefited everyone involved.

The Anne Hathaway movie, *The Intern* poignantly illustrates how generational gaps in the workplace can be bridged through mutual understanding and collaboration. In the film, a 65-year-old intern helps nurture the 30-year-old founder of a fast-paced startup, guiding her toward becoming the leader her company needs. As the founder learns to embrace the wisdom and experience of the intern, she gains invaluable insight into leadership, patience, and balance in her personal and professional life. Meanwhile, the intern adapts to the ever-evolving world of technology, learning from the younger generation's agility and innovation. The movie highlights that these generational differences need not be a source of division. Rather, they can become the foundation for a thriving, diverse work culture. It demonstrates that by promoting an environment where both younger and older employees can learn from one another, companies can bring out the best in every generation. We, too, can create such environments by encouraging collaboration, mutual respect, and a willingness to learn—empowering each generation to contribute in unique and valuable ways.

The need for effective communication between generations is also key to bridging the gap. Gen Z employees, having grown up with social media and instant messaging, are accustomed to quick, direct communication. They may find lengthy email chains or hierarchical approval processes cumbersome. To address this, managers can adopt more agile communication methods, such as regular one-on-one check-ins or team huddles. At the same time, younger employees should remain open to understanding the reasons behind certain processes and work towards finding common ground.

Recognition also plays a crucial role in enabling a cohesive workplace culture. While millennials may have been content with annual performance reviews, Gen Z thrives on immediate feedback. They want to know how they're doing in real-time so they can adjust their approach accordingly. Managers should consider incorporating regular feedback loops to keep their younger employees motivated and engaged. Companies can address this by clearly communicating their mission and values and showing how each employee's role aligns with these objectives. For instance, a company that prioritized sustainability found that its younger employees were more engaged and motivated when they saw tangible results from their efforts, such as reduced carbon emissions or increased community impact. This alignment of personal and organizational values can be a powerful driver of employee satisfaction and loyalty.

Companies can further bridge the gap by creating spaces for open dialogue. Town halls, focus groups, and anonymous feedback channels can give employees across generations a platform to voice their concerns and suggestions. For example, an organization once conducted a series of intergenerational workshops where employees shared their perspectives on workplace culture. The insights gathered from these sessions led to the implementation of policies that catered to the needs of both younger and older employees, such as flexible work arrangements and enhanced career development programs.

In conclusion, bridging the corporate generational gap in the workplace is not about changing one group to fit the mold of another, but about fostering understanding, adaptability, and collaboration. It requires effort from all the parties involved. Managers must embrace flexibility while providing guidance, and adapt adequate managerial styles depending on their reportees. Younger employees should balance their need for autonomy with a willingness to learn and communicate their needs while being open to feedback. Leadership must champion inclusivity and innovation while creating an environment that supports collaboration and mutual respect. HR teams, responsible for shaping policies that accommodate diverse work styles, must also play their part in fostering workplace harmony. Ultimately, when companies invest in open communication, continuous learning, and shared goals, generational differences become strengths rather than barriers. They not only enhance productivity but also build a culture of trust and innovation that benefits everyone. By embracing this shift, organizations can build a workplace culture that is not only more productive but also more dynamic, resilient, and future-ready.

About the Author

Vaishnavi Agrawal is a finance professional with a deep curiosity for understanding complex systems—whether in markets, businesses, or human behaviour. Armed with a strong analytical mindset and professional certifications in finance and risk management, she enjoys exploring the intersection of strategy, data, and decision-making. Throughout her career at top MNCs, she has worked with diverse teams, gaining insights into corporate structures, leadership styles, and the evolving nature of work. Beyond finance, she has a passion for creative storytelling, always seeking to make intricate concepts more accessible and engaging.

Her book, *Millennial Managers & Gen Z Employees*, is a reflection of her experiences navigating modern workplaces and observing generational shifts in expectations, work ethics, and leadership. Having worked closely with both experienced leaders and young professionals, she has seen how workplace cultures are evolving in real time. This book captures those changes, offering a fresh perspective on the modern workforce through a lens that is both analytical and deeply personal.

Whether you're a leader managing a new generation of employees, a young professional navigating corporate expectation, an HR strategist shaping workplace policies, an entrepreneur building a multi-generational team, or a student preparing to enter the workforce, this book provides the tools to bridge the gap. With sharp observations, real-world examples, and engaging storytelling, Vaishnavi unpacks the shifts shaping today's corporate world—offering valuable insights for anyone looking to understand, adapt, and thrive in the modern professional landscape.

Outside of work, Vaishnavi is an avid reader, writer, and painter. She finds inspiration in stories—whether in books, data, or the brushstrokes of her artwork. Always drawn to the patterns that shape decisions, relationships, and cultures, she enjoys unravelling complex ideas and expressing them through different creative mediums. With an insatiable curiosity and a drive to make sense of the changing world, she continues to explore, learn, and challenge perspectives—one conversation, one analysis, and one story at a time.

Bibliography

Mondo's article "*Latest Mass Layoffs: Detailed List & Reporting of Notable Company Cutbacks*" (Link) provides an in-depth analysis of recent layoffs across major industries, including technology, finance, and retail. It explores the impact of workforce reductions at companies like IBM, Amazon, Google, and Microsoft while discussing broader economic trends and the role of the Federal WARN Act in employee rights. Additionally, their report examines how layoffs in the tech sector contrast with overall job market resilience, highlighting emerging opportunities despite widespread downsizing.

The article titled "*Millennials or Gen Z: Who is doing the most job-hopping?*" (Link) examines job tenure differences among generations, highlighting that younger workers tend to change jobs more frequently than older cohorts. According to CareerBuilder data cited in the article, Generation Z (ages 6-24) spends an average of 2 years and 3 months in a job, while Millennials (ages 25-40) average 2 years and 9 months. In contrast, Generation X (ages 41-56) maintains an average tenure of 5 years and 2 months, and Baby

Boomers (ages 57-75) average 8 years and 3 months. The article attributes this trend among younger workers to a desire for better pay, benefits, flexibility, and a reassessment of personal priorities, especially in the wake of the COVID-19 pandemic.

The Business Insider article *"Gen Z is Happy to Job-Hop and Quit Without a Backup Plan, Survey Finds"* (Link) highlights findings from an Oliver Wyman survey that explores Gen Z's attitudes toward job stability. The survey reveals that a significant portion of Gen Z workers are comfortable quitting jobs without securing another, prioritizing mental well-being, flexibility, and work-life balance over traditional job security. Unlike previous generations, they are more willing to explore multiple career paths and seek roles that align with their personal values. The study suggests that employers need to adapt their retention strategies to accommodate Gen Z's expectations in the evolving job market.

Acknowledgments

This book would not have been possible without the incredible support and encouragement of so many people in my life.

To my **family**, thank you for being my constant source of strength. Your belief in me kept me grounded through every doubt and every late-night writing sprint.

To my **friends**, I'm grateful for your patience, your thoughtful insights, and for always being willing to listen—whether I was excitedly rambling or stuck in a creative block.

To my **colleagues,** thank you for sharing your experiences, and perspectives. Many of the ideas in this book were sparked by conversations with you.

And a special thank you to my **sister, Aditi**—your wisdom, clarity, and quiet strength have inspired me more than you know. Thank you for always showing up, in ways big and small, and for being one of my fiercest cheerleaders.

To everyone who's been part of this journey—thank you from the bottom of my heart.

www.ingramcontent.com/pod-product-compliance
Lightning Source LLC
LaVergne TN
LVHW041535070526
838199LV00046B/1682